NAVIGATING
Love

A Memoir of Rage,

Courage, and Becoming

DR. ROBIN MARTIN

Navigating Love

© 2025 Dr. Robin Martin

All rights reserved. No part of this book may be reproduced, stored in a retrieval system, or transmitted in any form or by any means—electronic, mechanical, photocopying, recording, or otherwise—without prior written permission of the publisher, except in the case of brief quotations used in reviews or critical articles.

First Edition: August 15, 2025

Library of Congress Control Number: 2025918560
ISBN: 979-8-9998372-0-2

Printed in the United States of America

Published by:
Robin Martin & Associates, LLC
Cincinnati, Ohio

Author: Dr. Robin Martin, Cincinnati, OH
Printing Partner: WorldPac Paper, LLC, Cincinnati, OH

For more information, visit: www.navigatingcourage.com

Dedication

To My Mother, Gladys P. Martin, and All Black Women:

The love we seek resides within thee.
In our laughter and in our rage,
in our scars and in our brilliance.
We are the Divine.

#navigatinglove

CONTENTS

Prelude: When The World Cracked Open 1

How To Read This Book 8

Introduction: A Love Story in Three Acts 11

Chapter 1: I Left My Good-Paying Job 17

Chapter 2: Rest Wasn't Rest 27

Chapter 3: Unraveling 35

Chapter 4: Navigating Courage Framework / Healing / Preparing For The Next Departure 43

Chapter 5: Sudden Departure 54

Chapter 6: Chosen Path, Love, and Freedom 60

Chapter 7: The Man From Dupont Circle 69

Chapter 8: The First Goodbye 79

Chapter 9: What Our Mothers Taught Us 88

Chapter 10: The Grief In The Yes 97

Chapter 11: Don't Leave Me While You're Still Here 108

Chapter 12: Tragic Fairy Encounter 115

Chapter 13: I Will Try My Best 123

Chapter 14: Benin — The Trip That Changed Everything130

Chapter 15: The Cigarette 135

Chapter 16: The Space Between Leaving and Becoming.. 142

A Memoir of Rage,
Courage, and Becoming

Prelude

WHEN THE WORLD CRACKED OPEN

This book began in 2020—the year the universe cracked wide open. A global pandemic collided with a racial reckoning, shaking the world's sense of normalcy and decency. As COVID-19 spread, claiming millions of lives, another pandemic unfolded in real time: the modern-day lynching of George Floyd, captured in a video that ignited the world.

I still remember the moment. Derek Chauvin's knee pressed into Floyd's neck for 8 minutes and 46 seconds. His cry— "Mama"—was a collective summons. A breaking point. A prayer. It stirred something ancient in us.

DR. ROBIN MARTIN

Black Lives Matter re-emerged, this time louder. Streets across continents filled with people chanting, grieving, raging. Corporate statements, foundation pledges, celebrity endorsements poured in like promises wrapped in urgency. Even the NFL raised a fist—after years of silence. For a moment, it felt like change might be coming.

But then, something familiar crept back in— silence.

Solidarity faded. Compassion gave way to conspiracy, as rugged individualism returned like a bad habit and public empathy gave way to private comfort. The promise of a shared humanity dissolved into every man for himself.

Outraged, I began walking. Writing. Remembering. I lived alone in Seattle, and in the stillness, I listened. To the ancestors. To the earth. To myself.

I began writing what I called "raging rants"—notes, poems, thoughts of the day. I let my rage speak because

I knew it would either consume me or free me. I chose freedom.

That choice led me back to my doctoral research on the African philosophy of Ubuntu: "I am because you are." I began crafting a framework to hold what I was feeling. It wasn't just a tool—it was a way to live. A humanist approach to healing, leading, and being in a world that seemed hell-bent on tearing us apart.

I named it the **Navigating Courage Framework**—a map for re-centering our humanity in the face of dehumanization. Here are the four guiding principles I developed and began to share:

Navigating Courage Framework: Principles In Practice

Be Human

The pursuit of deeper self-awareness and personal growth. It goes beyond surface-level self-reflection—it's a mindset rooted in self-discovery, critique, and continuous refinement. This is what I call the art of humanity—the ongoing exploration of self and others in the search for greater possibility. As we come to understand our own values, strengths, limitations, and complexities, only then can we begin to recognize and embrace the richness and complexity in others.

For me, *Be Human* is about directly acknowledging my own humanity—and committing to the internal work required for personal growth and transformation.

Be in Community

The second principle in the Navigating Courage Framework is *Be in Community / Interconnectedness.* When I began developing the framework, the core concept of Ubuntu—interconnectedness—forced me to confront the relationship between my personal growth and how I show up in community and relationships.

This principle requires trust, collaboration, and the inherent belief that real change and transformation happen with people, not of people. It disrupted my previous notions of individualism and meritocracy as viable solutions to economic, political, and social parity, instead underscoring the importance of communal relationships over individualistic pursuits.

Be Curious

This is a continuous, integrated, systems-level approach to personal, professional, and human advancement. It requires us to become critical thinkers, view critique as a source of innovation, and consistently challenge our own ways of knowing. It centers on exploring beyond the impulse to find the "right" answer—unlocking the limitless possibilities of knowing and being.

Be Curious is more than accepting diverse voices, creative ideas, and new perspectives—it's about relying on them. It rests on the foundational belief that we must reject every notion of exceptionalism and replace it with interdependence and deep curiosity.

Be Courageous

The ultimate principle of the Navigating Courage Framework is Courage itself. It's where the rubber meets the road. Courage is standing up for your beliefs in the face of fear, challenges, and opposition.

It involves strategically identifying your sphere of influence—understanding what is within your control, aligning it with your role, title, or responsibilities, and then taking deliberate action to effect change.

Be Courageous is about taking ownership of your actions, making conscious choices to lead with intention, and using your individual and collective power—however big or small—to challenge and transform oppressive systems.

NAVIGATING LOVE

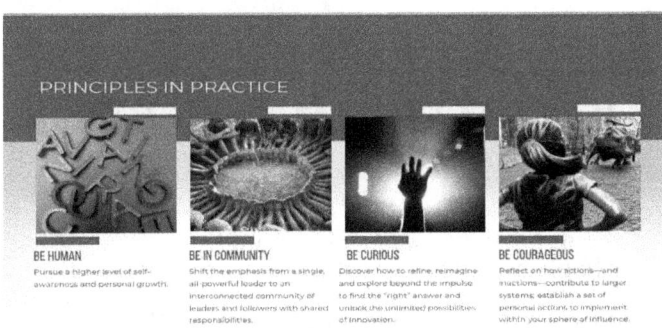

HOW TO READ THIS BOOK

This book is a tapestry of stories—personal reflections, poems, and what I call courageous thoughts. Think of it as a mixtape—rhythms and truths designed to provoke reflection, spark courage, and inspire action.

Storytelling is my art form. While others may paint or sculpt, I make sense of life through words. It's how I sort fact from fiction, truth from lies, and clarity from chaos. As a trained researcher and consultant, I developed the Navigating Courage Framework to anchor my journey toward personal growth, interconnectedness, and intentional living.

The following stories are not exactly arranged chronologically, nor do they follow a linear path. Instead, they reflect the messiness of life—a nonlinear exploration of what it means to be fully human. They examine how I show up in the world, how I lead, and how I heal.

Each chapter ends with a *Courage Reflection*—a poem, passage, or personal affirmation—or a *Courage Card™*, a simple reminder of personal power, possibility, and connection within a supportive community. Together, they offer wisdom and inspiration to help foster resilience and courage in everyday life.

At its core, this book is about humanity, rage, and courage. These principles are the foundation of every artist, every creator. I believe artists, in their purest form, are attempting to articulate the divine—expressing the humanity of God, the chaos of creation, and the courage it takes to share their gifts with the world. This work is my attempt to do just that.

So I invite you to reflect on how our individual and collective actions either sustain or disrupt the world

DR. ROBIN MARTIN

we live in. My hope is that you see yourself as a co-creator of your own life.

Welcome to the Journey!

Introduction

A LOVE STORY IN THREE ACTS

This book is the first in a three-part *Navigating Courage* series—*Navigating Love, Navigating Leadership,* and *Navigating Workplace Culture.* Each explores a different dimension of the human experience, but all are rooted in the same question: **What does it mean to lead with humanity in a complicated world?**

This volume, *Navigating Love*, is a love story. But not the kind you find in Hallmark cards.

It's about caring for aging parents while trying to build a life. It's about the messy intersections of identity, freedom, family, and romance. It's about loving a man while grieving a mother. It's about rage as a form of clarity, and courage as a practice—not a performance.

At the heart of it all is a deep reckoning—with who I've been, who I'm becoming, and the legacy of love and loss that has shaped me. And like so many of our love stories, mine begins with my mother.

My Mother's Story

A single mother of four children from four different men, she gladly accepted the challenge and responsibility of raising us. Necessity turned into pride, pride into survival, and survival into normal.

Not having a man in the house became, in some strange way, her way of protecting us—and herself. It wasn't just a circumstance; it was a way of life.

I will never fully understand, nor be able to tell, her whole story. Like most of our stories, my mother's story is a puzzle pieced together from fragments—half-truths, unbearable truths, and truths reshaped to protect, to forget, and sometimes, simply to endure.

My clearest window into her life came through the stories she told again and again—memorized accounts etched as deeply into our memories as they were into hers. The one story she repeated most was about her abusive father—my grandfather.

She described the constant physical abuse he inflicted on her mother (my grandmother), the instability he created, the constant moves from house to house and school to school, never knowing when or how the next disruption would come. She spoke of her hatred for him and of the ways she and her younger sister plotted to hurt him to protect their mother.

Her most vivid story was the day she and her sister finally stood up to him—older now, braver—threatening to kill him if he ever touched their mother again. I remember the look in her eyes when she told it:

rage and courage tangled together, with a fierce pride that they had fought back.

So, when she turned 18 years old and left her father's house, I often wondered if she made a deliberate choice to avoid having men in her home. I will never know whether she refused to love or simply never found it. Either way, I grew up in a household where a man was never present—nor did I feel the absence. It was like breathing. You don't notice it. You can't miss what you've never known. Yet later, I would learn just how deeply that absence shaped me.

My Father's Love

I was lucky. Out of four children, I was the one who had a relationship with my father, even though he and my mother were never together. Every other summer, I would visit him and spend time getting to know his side of the family.

My father was a good man—the kind who loved me without question, perhaps without fully knowing me. I was his only child. His baby girl. His superstar. We didn't live together, so I loved him from afar, yet felt deeply close when I was in his presence.

Sometimes, absence paints the most generous portraits.

Like my mother, he also told stories over and over—except his stories were often about me. He bragged about his daughter to anyone who would listen. He didn't have to say he loved me; I felt it every time I was near him. Being with him was like stepping into a warm, secure place—a place I will always be grateful for.

The Reckoning

My mother's path with me was different. She raised me, fed me, and fought for me. She was larger than life—wise, pragmatic, unflinching. I thought I knew her. But when she moved in with me after the COVID-19 pandemic, I began to see her fully—her rhythms, her fears, her brilliance, and her limitations.

DR. ROBIN MARTIN

Caring for her was both an honor and a reckoning. So much of my strength comes from her—and so much of my struggle. She was my mirror, reflecting what I had inherited and what I still needed to heal.

This book begins there—in the space between goodbye and becoming. Between caring for a parent and choosing a partner. Between grief and grace.

Because somewhere along the way, I met a man who reminded me that love could feel like home. And in choosing to build a life with him, I understood something fundamental:

My freedom was always tied to hers.

Chapter 1

I LEFT MY GOOD-PAYING JOB

I left my good-paying job.

I remember waking up in the middle of the night—sleepless, exhausted, and full of questions. After months of working 12-hour days, eating canned sardines three nights a week, and praying for clarity, I started searching. Searching for how best to use my gifts and talents in this moment.

From the outside, everything looked perfect. I was at the top of my professional game, but something deep inside me was shifting. Whether it was the universe or just my own intuition, I knew I needed a break.

DR. ROBIN MARTIN

This wasn't just about COVID-19, or even the ongoing, state-sanctioned violence that has always haunted Black and Brown people in this country. It was something deeper. Lurking behind work meetings, coffee chats, and the speeches of powerful people was something unmistakable: Fear. You could hear it in the tremble of voices, feel it in the tension on Zoom calls, and see it in the eyes of leaders grasping for control.

George Floyd's murder sparked a firestorm—Rage, Courage, and yes, more Fear. COVID drew new lines in the social hierarchy, dividing us into "essential" and "non-essential" workers. While millions died and the country spiraled, we were told to prove our worth. Prove we were essential. Perform harder. Push through. Be grateful. Be visible—but not too much.

Fear was the loudest voice in every room, reminding us that anyone could be next— laid off, hospitalized, or worse. Even the privilege of working from home didn't shield us from the toxicity building around us; it only disguised it for a while.

NAVIGATING LOVE

That fear lingered long after the calls ended, pressing me to question not just the environment around me but the one I had also created within myself. It takes courage to set personal boundaries in a capitalist society that constantly demands boundless production, time, and effort. The system of more has no bottom. During the first year of the pandemic, I watched as businesses and the U.S. government allowed millions to die, and I began to reflect on my own unhealthy relationship with work—60+ hour weeks, back-to-back meetings, and the idea that every moment needed to be productive.

I recall when leadership decided we'd end meetings ten minutes before the hour so we could take a bio break. Yes, you heard me—we had to schedule time to pee.

I watched colleagues break down. I saw the cracks form—mental, physical, emotional. And I saw how corporations responded: with more demands. More output. More pressure.

DR. ROBIN MARTIN

In some strange way, seeing the carnage and senseless deaths while working in a place of privilege and power—high salaries, prestige, the perception of influence—forced me to reject compartmentalization. I could no longer pretend that my work and my humanity lived in separate rooms.

Like many people, I had been taught to split myself into manageable pieces. Career in one box. Emotions in another. Family, friends, rage, dreams—all neatly shelved. "Everything in decency and order," my family used to say. It meant: control yourself. Stay composed. Be professional, even amid the trauma.

But when we disconnect from what's happening around us, we also disconnect from ourselves. And that disconnect is the root of bigotry, apathy, classism, and more. If we refuse to see our interconnection, we miss the opportunity to act courageously.

So, after the "not guilty" verdict in Breonna Taylor's case, I lay in bed for hours, weeping. For the first time

NAVIGATING LOVE

in a long time, I gave myself permission to stop pretending I was okay. I chose to grieve. To feel. To care for myself. I began silently reevaluating my unsustainable worship of a job, a title, a version of success built on sacrifice and silence. And I realized: I could not keep pretending that the line between my rage and my labor didn't exist.

Once I shredded the idea of compartmentalization, I tapped into something much greater than status or salary—I tapped into purpose. I began to see work as a side hustle to my real life.

Because here's the truth: corporations aren't designed to protect your humanity. The system is not designed to see you. It's your responsibility—our responsibility—to see ourselves, and care for ourselves.

So, after the holidays, I made the decision: I left the good-paying job.

DR. ROBIN MARTIN

I knew the work I was doing wasn't essential—not in the way the world had redefined it. It was important, yes. But not enough to sacrifice my health, my peace, my sense of purpose. Maybe I was afraid, too. Maybe it was fear that finally pushed me away. Or maybe I simply couldn't bear to watch an organization with so much power and influence squander a moment that demanded boldness.

Even as I gave my notice, I knew how it would be received. I wrote the letter. I thanked the team. I acknowledged all the growth, the lessons, and the memories. But when a Black woman decides to walk away from power, on her own financial terms, it rattles people. It rattles the system. Rumors floated, speculation spread. Some didn't believe it. Some didn't like it.

But I was clear: I needed to breathe.

So I wrote:

NAVIGATING LOVE

After a period of deep reflection, I am excited to share with you all that I will be leaving. My time here has brought so many blessings—and a lot of good work—into my life.

As I thought about how to say this, I kept returning to the words of Audre Lorde: "Sometimes we drag ourselves with dreams of new ideas. The head will save us. The brain alone will set us free. But there are no new ideas waiting in the wings to save us as women, as humans. There are only old and forgotten ones, new combinations, extrapolations, and recognitions from within ourselves–along with the renewed courage to try them out."

I told the team that my departure was rooted in a yearning to explore those old and forgotten ideas, to reimagine what a full life could look like—and to do so with the renewed Courage to try them out.

Two weeks after I left, I welcomed myself home again. For the first time in my adult life, I gave myself permission to take a break—a real break. No children. No partner. No deadlines. Just space. COVID had taken its toll. And working at one of the largest philanthropic institutions in the world had drained every last bit of energy I had.

For three years, I had pushed myself—driven by purpose, fueled by possibility. I made more money than I ever had before. But none of it could quiet the voice in my head whispering, *This is not it.*

I couldn't always explain my decision to others. I just knew I needed to be free. Even if just for a moment. I needed time to return to myself. To rest. To reset.

So, I stepped away. Back in my own home, I was finally resting. Planning to travel, to move freely, to reconnect with joy. For the first time in years, I allowed myself to breathe.

And then—two weeks after I left my good-paying job—my mother destabilized and unhoused herself and

NAVIGATING LOVE

called me to solve it. It was the same familiar dance she and I had taken over the past thirty years.

Welcome back home.

DR. ROBIN MARTIN

COURAGE CARD

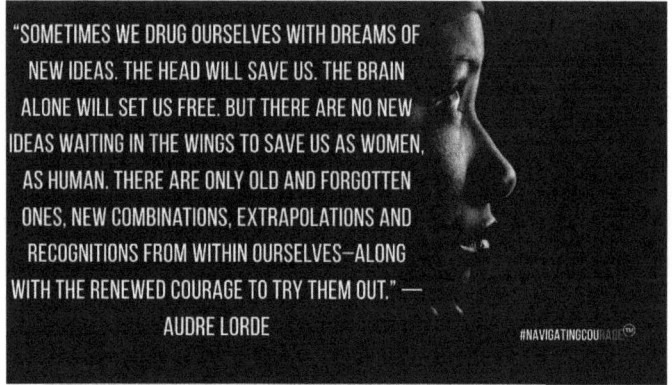

Chapter 2

REST WASN'T REST

It had been years since my mother last lived with me. This was our third stint living together. The starts and stops had become a familiar cycle: apartment to apartment, house to house, short stays with friends, temporary spaces with family. The moves were too numerous to count. With each one, things got left behind—family heirlooms, paperwork, medical records, pieces of a life. All of it slowly disappearing.

Leaving and starting over had become an addiction. Not just for her, but for those of us, mostly her children, who were constantly picking up the pieces. Move quickly. Stabilize. Keep it moving—until the next move.

DR. ROBIN MARTIN

One day, I counted. Twelve moves over the course of seven years.

Before she moved back into my house this time, I don't think I ever really saw her—not all the way. I saw the imagined version of her. The version I needed to believe in. The hero. The provider. But I hadn't seen the trauma—layered deep behind every relationship, every job that didn't last, every period of silence, every sudden move. I didn't see the weight she was carrying until it spilled all over me.

The first few months were a blur of appointments. Stabilizing her became my full-time job—doctors' visits, Medicaid paperwork, haircuts, new clothes, even pedicures. What was supposed to be my time on bed rest quickly dissolved into chaos. In that moment, once again, I was the caretaker—the childless parent of the parent.

Through it all, she wore her familiar smile. The nurses and receptionists adored her, just as they always had.

NAVIGATING LOVE

At the eye clinic, it was no different—she was a star, charming everyone from the front desk to the medical assistants. That part of her never changed.

The doctors' visits brought back memories—hard ones. Years earlier, in Knoxville, we sat in Dr. Smith's office. He was a kind man, gentle but direct. Together with his father, he had built one of the largest optometry and glaucoma practices in the city.

After running all the tests, he walked back into the room wearing a look I'll never forget—the look of someone who hated delivering bad news.

"Ms. Martin, you have aggressive glaucoma in your left eye. You're losing vision quickly. We need to schedule surgery right away."

We sat in silence.

As always, I snapped into action. Pulled out my phone, opened my calendar. Started figuring out what days I could take off work so I could be there when she had surgery.

DR. ROBIN MARTIN

But when we got to the front desk to schedule the surgery, she paused.

"We'll call you back," she told them.

We never scheduled that surgery.

Now, sitting beside her again—years later—in another office, I watched her take the eye exam.

The right eye did fine. She read most of the chart. Not bad for a 79-year-old woman.

Then the left eye.

She put the patch over her right eye.

"What letters do you see?" the assistant asked.

"I can't see anything."

Next line.

"I can't see anything."

Again.

NAVIGATING LOVE

"No. I can't see the screen."

My heart broke in real time.

She was completely blind in her left eye.

And all I could hear was Dr. Smith's voice: *If you don't have the surgery, you will lose your vision.*

We left the appointment with two prescriptions to lower the pressure in the right eye. The doctor was optimistic. If we stayed on top of things, she could preserve some of the vision in the right eye. She started taking the drops. The pressure came down.

Next came depression and high blood pressure. We found a wonderful primary care doctor—kind, patient, and most importantly, he listened. Really listened. She felt seen, and she left that appointment feeling better.

The medications worked. Her mood stabilized. The anxiety quieted. Her blood pressure dropped. Her energy returned. She started to care again—about her hair, her feet, and her clothes. New shoes. A couple of new outfits. A little light returned.

DR. ROBIN MARTIN

I hadn't even noticed how much time had passed since I left my job and when she had moved in with me until a friend called me one day.

"What have you been doing with your time since you left your job?" she asked.

We talked, and she mentioned needing help on a project. That call pulled me back in. That same day, I decided to restart my consulting practice.

I looked around and realized my so-called 'adult gap year' had quietly shrunk to barely two weeks of rest. Still, all things considered, life seemed to be moving in the right direction. I was working again. I was writing. And she was stable.

Until—she relapsed.

She stopped the eye drops. Told herself she didn't have high blood pressure. Skipped the depression meds.

I didn't know what to do.

I was scared. For her. For me.

NAVIGATING LOVE

I had starred in this movie before. And no matter how many times I tried to rewrite the ending—tried to unsee what was right in front of me—the story kept playing out the same way.

And then, just like that, she came undone.

And so did I.

DR. ROBIN MARTIN

COURAGE CARD

Chapter 3

UNRAVELING

I walked into the kitchen and saw it—that spirit of depression and trauma creeping back in. She had stopped combing her hair. Stopped bathing. Refused her meds. That familiar, unsparing monster had returned—and this time, it was holding tight.

From the outside, she looked healthy enough. But I knew better. The untreated depression. The heart issues. The blindness in one eye. Even the good days felt fragile.

We began to argue over small things. Then came the silence—the hardest part. It felt like losing my best friend at the very moment I needed her most.

DR. ROBIN MARTIN

'Do you remember the last time you lived with me? I was working 60-hour weeks at the university while also pursuing my doctorate full-time. I don't remember what brought you back to my home that time, but I needed the help. You were younger then—still moving, still doing. We had a rhythm. I washed the clothes, and you folded them. I cooked; you did the dishes. On weekends, we cleaned together. I truly don't think I would have made it through that final year of studies without you.'

And then, she left again.

This time was different. I was different.

After leaving my job, I made a promise to be present in my own life—to truly see myself. That, I realized, was the greatest gift 2020 gave me. I chose to reprioritize, to radically shift the way I was living.

As the days passed and life became more complicated, I felt something breaking open inside me—and inside her, too. That's when I began to notice the rage.

NAVIGATING LOVE

I began to write: personal notes, short stories, essays, "thoughts of the day," and what I called "raging rants." Writing has always been my lifeline, the only way to make sense of the weight pressing down on me. It forced me to listen deeply, to feel love and pain, joy and anger—to rediscover myself.

I began writing because I didn't know what else to do. I wrote to stay human. To stay alive. To hold on to something—anything—that reminded me I still belonged to this world. And in doing that, I began to see more clearly. I saw her. I saw myself. I saw the system.

The tension between us grew. Arguments over eye drops, pills, and even simple things like taking a bath became daily battles. My relationships with siblings and other family members were also frayed. I heard whispers—rumors that she was planning to leave again. Every time she destabilized herself, she destabilized me—she destabilized us.

DR. ROBIN MARTIN

I started raging. And instinctively, I knew the rage was consuming me.

The universe had finally sat me down long enough to see everything for what it really was—and it was terrifying.

So I turned back to the only thing I've ever trusted with my truth: writing. My rage portal. A space to scream, cuss, fight, reflect, meditate, and sometimes—heal.

Sitting in my office one day, I wrote:

"Entangled in the Storm"

When did I become entangled in the web of your trauma?

When did the suffocating grip of depression shift from your being to mine?

Desperately maneuvering to evade another blow, I find myself consumed by rage after yet another unsuccessful battle.

Fuck.

NAVIGATING LOVE

I vowed I would not allow this cycle to repeat. This burden is yours to bear, not mine. Not this time.

Fuck.

Once again, I allowed it to seep into my being. As you fight for your own survival, I find myself fighting for mine. It is an unfair fight—why should it even be a fight at all?

More rage stirs within me, followed by moments of silence, prayer, anger, and anxiety. Then more prayer to seek solace.

Fuck.

Exhausted and drained, I plead to God—please release me from this relentless rollercoaster ride.

Fuck.

Here it comes again.

Fuck

DR. ROBIN MARTIN

I continued to write:

"AR-15: An Awakening of Self"

You were wrong today, and I just dug in– weaponizing my intellectual prowess– shots firing like an AR 15 destroying any sliver of logic. I was right you were wrong I repeat in my head justifying the assault excusing the heavy-handed arsenal. I was right, you see.

I walk away proud to be right, standing on principle yet failing to demonstrate decency and any measure of humanity. Then suddenly my mind, body and soul reconnected to the universe for just one split second, long enough to whisper – "are you right."

"Are you alright?"

I begin to cry.

No, I am not alright. I am not right.

It's the first time I see my own soul. My own humanity.

I was wrong today.

NAVIGATING LOVE

I finally see Me.

Days turned into months. I watched my anger turn to rage, to grief, to love—then back to anger, to confusion, and rage again. The weight of it felt like a storm I couldn't escape, while trying to hold myself together and care for my mother, whose spirit seemed trapped in another body. A spirit I didn't know. A spirit that didn't seem to know me either.

Work, clean, care for her, write, sleep—that was my routine. My so-called professional gap year was officially over, and there I stood—grateful I could care for her in this season, and resentful that I had to. Especially like this.

Hell, she wasn't even nice.

DR. ROBIN MARTIN

COURAGE REFLECTION

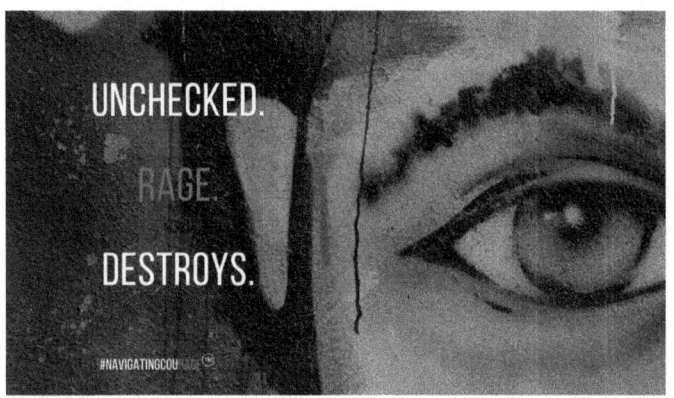

Chapter 4

NAVIGATING COURAGE FRAMEWORK / HEALING / PREPARING FOR THE NEXT DEPARTURE

I vividly recall one day trying to get her to take her eye drops. She refused. I tried to explain why they were necessary. She didn't care. Frustrated, I left the house and drove around for hours, finally landing at the neighborhood park behind our home. I watched the kids play. I called a friend. I listened to music.

In essence, I had unhoused myself—running from the pain inside my own home.

I continued to write and rage.

"Playing with a Raging Sword"

The power of rage is a double-edged sword. It can fight for love and, at times, spew venomous destruction when pain is present.

Today, I find myself raging against my family. These are the very people the universe has tasked me to journey through life with. I'm raging against the hurt, pain, confusion, and deceit. I'm raging against the lies. And while it's easier to rage against them, today I challenge myself to confront how my own rage has also caused hurt, pain, confusion, deceit—and even lies.

Today, I lean into the sharp, bloody edge of the sword, not suppressing my rage, but tasting the blood in the back of my throat.

I continued to write:

NAVIGATING LOVE

"The Master"

She mastered the face of strength—smiling to pretend everything was okay. Never letting anyone really know the truth. At times, she hated me because she knew I knew. She knew I could see—forcing her to push me far away. I was the last light she would see, would reject, deep down, love and loathe at the same time.

She held on until the end—her way, her time, her decisions—even the bad ones. Control became the purpose of life, not living. I wish I understood it. My attempts, my need to understand it, at times, felt like it would cost me my own life.

I wonder what being in control meant to her.

Was it learned? Survival?

Either way, its hardened grip created an unfree life— unworthy of her beautiful soul.

In you, I pray I learn to let go—forsake the need for all-consuming control. Learn how to live, to be, to love freely without the fear of someone seeing the full me.

DR. ROBIN MARTIN

I pray this lesson is not repeated in our family again. For you have paid the price for all of us.

So I thank you and damn you at the same time. I wanted a different life for you. I wanted to control what that life could look like, feel like, and be like. But you had your own plans—your way.

Today, I honor that strength. I curse that strength. And more importantly, I accept that strength. For I will never understand where it originated—learned or survival. Either way, I raise my cup to the Master.

That park became my safe space.

But the grief was relentless. I sank into depression and finally decided to get counseling. After just three counseling sessions, something began to shift. Speaking out loud, journaling, and my daily escapes to the park gave me enough space to re-ground myself. To catch my breath.

I pulled out my old journals and a manuscript I had been working on titled *A New Rage Is Needed in the*

NAVIGATING LOVE

World. It was the seed of what would become the **Navigating Courage Framework**—rooted in humanity, rage, and courage.

In those pages, I returned to my old academic notes on the African philosophy of Ubuntu: *I am because you are.* More than an idea, Ubuntu is a way of being—centering human dignity, mutual responsibility and the truth that our lives are bound together.

As I reimagined these principles as humanist constructs, I realized my rage—my outrage—was always rooted in love. Love for people. Love for justice. Love for her. That combination—rage and love—produced courage. It pushed me beyond the fear that kept me from truly seeing her and, just as importantly, seeing myself.

Be Human. Be In Community. Be Curious. Be Courageous.

What began as theory was no longer abstract. These were living truths. I knew I had to stop theorizing and start applying—turning research into practice.

DR. ROBIN MARTIN

Implementing the Navigating Courage Principles

While she was still with me, I committed to living into the framework in real time:

Be Human — Every day, I started with mental, emotional, and physical check-ins. I'd ask myself one question: *What do you need to be fully human today?* The answer changed daily. Some days it meant exercising. Others, an extra-long shower, cooking a special breakfast, scrolling through social media, or simply turning back over in bed for 15 more minutes of sleep or meditation.

This practice went beyond how people talk about "self-care." I was prioritizing my needs first—in real time. It created space for me to be fully present with myself. To create belonging for my emotional and physical needs. And it wasn't just in my personal life—I began to re-prioritize (and sometimes de-prioritize) everything: friendships, work, and community. That was revolutionary for me.

NAVIGATING LOVE

As a Black woman who'd always been celebrated for being a "good laborer," someone who "gets shit done," the act of Being Human—of slowing down to check in with myself—was quietly radical. It forced me to turn away from the outside world and toward myself.

Be in Community / Interconnectedness — Once I committed to seeing and honoring my own humanity, I turned my attention to what it meant to be in community with her—my mother. My hero. Or, at times, the spiraling spirit that steeped through the cavity of her upper torso like a haunting shadow.

I never knew which version of her I would meet each day, but after I did my own work, I found I could meet her exactly where she was—regardless.

Each morning, after my rituals, I'd ask myself: *How do I want to show up in this relationship today?* Eventually, I had to admit that I was part of the problem, too. That if we were going to survive this moment, I needed to take responsibility for my own rage, my own judgments, and my own actions.

DR. ROBIN MARTIN

We were connected. Interconnected. And when I was off—when I was struggling with my own mental health—my toxicity leaked into her world. So each day I'd ask: *What energy are you bringing into this space, and how are your actions or inactions shaping this relationship?*

Be Curious — This was the hard one. Because I had to unlearn the need to be right.

You see, for a poor Black girl raised in a patriarchal and racist world that constantly tries to prove you wrong, being right becomes the highest form of self-worth. Being right becomes your God.

So, I walked around being right.

The most difficult part of practicing this framework was letting go of certainty, of control, of being "correct."

However, once I released that grip, I started to listen more and asked more questions. In letting go, I discovered that listening was its own kind of freedom—an opening that drew me closer to her.

She and I would sit for hours. She'd tell me the same stories, again and again. And I listened. I asked new questions. I leaned in.

In those stories, I began to see her more clearly. I started to understand what she was really trying to say—what her repetition was trying to reveal. Not just about her, but about me.

I began to understand why she always felt more comfortable being unhoused. It was how she grew up. Her family moved from house to house, never feeling at ease when my abusive grandfather was around. Stability was never something she or her siblings had. Stability wasn't a luxury afforded to her and her siblings —it was an illusion. Being unhoused wasn't a breakdown. It was a return to the only version of home she had ever known.

Be Courageous — That understanding helped me clarify what was within my sphere of control and what wasn't—when to take action, when to step in, and when to let go.

Often, the most courageous thing I could do was to be present: to listen, to provide her basic needs, and to love her unconditionally.

She needed me to see her—without judgment. To love her—without limits. To simply be her daughter, and at times, her friend.

That was hard, because everything in me wanted to fix it. Fix *her*. But I learned that courage wasn't about fixing. Courage was holding space—letting her be who she was, and letting myself be who I was.

COURAGE CARD

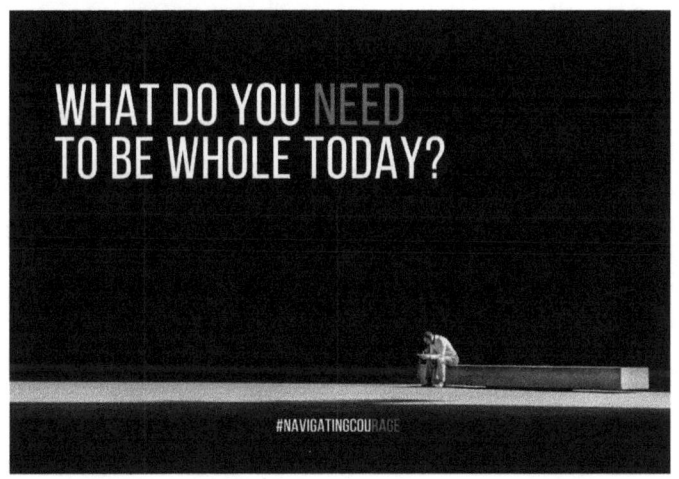

Chapter 5

SUDDEN DEPARTURE

I had finally started to get back on track. Settling into the new business and feeling more confident that leaving the job and restarting my consulting practice was the right decision.

Then she suddenly moved out again.

Another heart-wrenching and abrupt departure. After a few good weeks of laughter, shared meals, and an incredible five-hour car ride to visit family, everything turned chaotic before I left for my final work trip of the year.

I had continued putting the framework into practice:

NAVIGATING LOVE

Be Human:

Caregiving can swallow you whole. You can lose yourself in the lives of others. I had to remind myself daily to see my own humanity—my virtues, my flaws, my contradictions. I had to grant myself grace, the right to be imperfect, and space for self-care.

Be in Community / Interconnectedness:

I discovered the indispensable value of community. I had to see my mother, my family, our extended relatives, and even her medical care team as part of an interconnected web. Understanding their humanity, acknowledging their roles, and recognizing their shared commitment towards her well-being broadened my perspective.

Be Curious:

Putting this framework into practice, I began to embrace uncertainty and fully embrace that I didn't have all the answers. Curiosity became my anchor in constant change.

Be Courageous:

As caregivers, our natural inclination is to "fix" or solve the problem. However, over time, I realized that most things my mother was experiencing, I simply could not fix or solve for her. I couldn't undo the abuse or pain she experienced as a child at the hands of my grandfather, and how that trauma manifested in her behaviors and emotional response to certain situations. I couldn't fix her feelings of loneliness or yearning for a soulmate. I simply could not fill that void for her. Over time, I began to distinguish what was in and out of my sphere of influence and took the appropriate actions.

Let me be clear here– this takes courage. It means recognizing the fine line between supporting someone and carrying a weight that isn't yours to bear. That said, this simple, yet powerful mental shift allowed me to

NAVIGATING LOVE

quickly identify real and immediate actions I could take without losing sight of myself amidst the swirling vortex of responsibilities. My humanity had to be sustained alongside the care I extended to my mother.

And just like that, she was gone. I was left devastated.

She would return once more, in search of that warm, familiar place she called home—her good friend, Destabilization.

The details are still confusing. I don't fully understand why she left or why she didn't return. It was always unclear—when she arrived and when she left. Family confusion. Everyone involved. No one responsible.

The whispered conversations about her leaving my house had come true—like a psychic prediction.

Months before she left my house, I had told several family members that if she left this time, I wouldn't take her back in. Not because I didn't love her. But because I had begun to see the pattern as an addiction—one that was draining us all. I made a promise to myself: if

DR. ROBIN MARTIN

she left again, I would discontinue playing a part in the cycle.

I had made a commitment to care for her for the rest of her life. But not at the cost of my own. We were all strapped into a 50-year rollercoaster that had become unsafe for anyone to ride.

It almost cost me my life.

So, when she left this time, I made the hard choice. I would not return this place. And neither would she.

COURAGE CARD

Chapter 6

CHOSEN PATH, LOVE, AND FREEDOM

I dedicated my first book, *Navigating Courage: Leading Beyond Fear*, to my mother. In it, I wrote:

"Thank you for allowing me to live a free life to choose my path, learn from my mistakes, and own my excellence. Thank you for fostering an environment where my voice was heard, my questions were valid, and my 'sass' was both honored and tempered when needed. The truth is, I have never accomplished any meaningful task without your guidance and love. All of my life's successes are wrapped in the protection of your prayers and love. I thank God that he gave you the strength to give me birth,

NAVIGATING LOVE

the wisdom to guide my steps, and, more importantly, the courage to let me be me. All mothers give birth; you gave me Freedom."

In deeper reflection, so much of that dedication still rings true. But in this moment, what stands out most are the words: Chosen Path, Love, and Freedom.

Chosen Path

When she left, I felt like a failure. I questioned everything. Had I done something to make her leave? Had I made her feel unwanted or unloved? That guilt turned quickly to anger—not just toward her, but towards the whole family.

Her trauma, her addiction, her patterns—they were contagious. They were never contained. Like the Mississippi River, they moved with force, carrying debris from home to home, picking up more damage along the way. Contaminating us all.

DR. ROBIN MARTIN

It was late fall. The holidays were approaching. The house was quiet. The family fractured. Shattered into six micro-pieces. No one could really explain what had happened. It felt like a bomb had gone off, and I was walking around with shrapnel lodged in my heart.

So I made a decision. When she left, I decided to leave too. Not the house this time—but the family.

If she was the drug, I was the drug dealer. I funded every move. Solved every crisis. Offered every solution—even before they were asked for. I ran to everyone's rescue like a panting dog chasing a whistle no one blew.

But this time was different. I stopped. I let the silence stay. I sat with the pain. And I chose to *Be Human*. I stopped hiding. I let myself feel it all—the exhaustion, the resentment, the loneliness, even the rage.

The rage was loud and real. And when I finally stopped denying it, something shifted.

NAVIGATING LOVE

I gave my rage a home. I stopped pretending it didn't exist. I made room for it in my body, my mind, my spirit. And for the first time, I faced it fully—unfiltered, undiluted. And in doing so, I started to heal.

I stopped focusing so much on her—her trauma, her addiction—and turned inward. I began to look at my own trauma, my own addiction. I realized I was addicted to fixing—to the constant yearning to be needed, to control everything and everyone.

And in that space, the framework—*Be Human, Be in Community, Be Curious, Be Courageous*—became more than a mantra. It became my map.

I reflected on how I showed up in the family. How my trauma intertwined with theirs.

And I chose to change course. I chose healing. I chose myself.

DR. ROBIN MARTIN

Love

I took a long solo trip to another country. Not to escape, but to process. To breathe. I landed in Vancouver.

Before I left, I called a good friend who shares my love of food. I asked for recommendations. He sent me a list—and one strong suggestion: go to the spa in the forest.

"You'll find healing in that space," he said.

I hadn't told him what had happened, so I didn't fully understand what he meant. But he was right.

At that spa, surrounded by quiet trees and warm water, I started to forgive myself.

Yes, I'm a control freak. Yes, I've been a people pleaser. Yes, I've avoided boundaries I should have held firm. All of that is true.

But what's also true: I am a giver. I've made sacrifices most wouldn't even consider. I've shown up. I've stayed. I've loved beyond measure.

NAVIGATING LOVE

I started to see myself again—not the curated version, but the real me. What I discovered amidst the quiet trees was that I still loved her. I still loved me.

The day before I flew back, my brother called. He asked about your medications, old doctors, and how to navigate Medicaid. He and his wife were now in the cycle—hair appointments, new clothes, resettling.

I sat on the edge of my hotel bed and cried.

Before I left the hotel, I packed my bags and wrote the following words:

I forgive you. I forgive myself. I forgive the family. I choose love.

In some strange way, seeing myself clearly—owning all of it—reawakened my love for her.

So I wrote:

I love and will always love you for exactly who you are. You are the greatest human I know. Your laughter, your silly ways, your brilliance. You would give me the shirt off your back. I have always loved you. You have always loved me. We are the same.

Freedom

A month passed. No contact.

Then I called. She answered like nothing had happened. And I played along.

We never talked about the situation or what happened.

As the year ended, I started clearing the house. Packing up her things. It wasn't about spite. It was about closure. The rage had softened. It was no longer pulsing through my veins like fuel.

Something else had taken its place: Courage.

I was ready to choose my own path. To make my own decisions. To rediscover how to love me.

And as I folded the last shirt and closed the last box, I found myself whispering the words from that old book dedication—the one I now understood more fully than ever:

"I thank God that he gave you the strength to give me birth, the wisdom to guide my steps, and, more importantly, the courage to let me be me. All mothers give birth; you gave me Freedom."

DR. ROBIN MARTIN

COURAGE REFLECTION

It takes courage to navigate family dynamics—those relationships that society tells us should be a "special bond." Navigating your individual journey within the family unit is incredibly challenging. It's complicated. It's something that both troubles our souls and brings us joy. Family has the power to both cripple and nourish, destroy and uplift, bring riches and deplete. Family is never neatly wrapped up. It is the one aspect of life that requires a high degree of navigational skills and a reliable compass. Because let's face it, it's the one area in our lives where the destination is unclear, and the promises of riches at the end are often never realized until it's too late.

Chapter 7

THE MAN FROM DUPONT CIRCLE

Just when I was stable, the man from Dupont Circle showed up.

A new year, a new season, and a new me. I started the year fully immersed in building my consulting practice—with renewed focus and the assurance that I had made the right decision to leave my job two years ago. It was hard to imagine that two years had passed, but I was gaining momentum.

Single for a long time, just before I met him, I had gone out with several other men, testing to see if any were worth my time. I was a lone wolf, free to roam as I pleased—unencumbered—so I started dating again.

They seemed fine, but I was looking for peace—and a grown-ass man. The past few years had been difficult, and I was not about to invite difficulty back into my life. I was still practicing the framework: Be Human, Be in Community, Be Curious, and Be Courageous. I was focused on myself, really paying attention to who was in my community, asking a lot of questions, and—more importantly—taking swift action. I was on a roll.

The dating scene was both frightening and liberating. I dated on my terms. It allowed me to practice, to refine, and to clearly articulate my needs, desires, and dreams for the person I wanted in my life. One by one, I asked each of them to leave. I was both calm and clear about what I needed at this moment—even though I didn't know where to find it. I just knew.

The month before I met him, I was in Washington, D.C., celebrating with my college roommates. I was there for

NAVIGATING LOVE

work, but as luck would have it, I joined my colleagues and longtime friends. Food, fun, high fashion, and the joy of being surrounded by some of the most incredible Black women I know. We had a magical time.

Two weeks later, I was back in D.C. for another work assignment with my former employer—now as a subcontractor, doing the work I love. What a blessing. Never in my wildest dreams could I have imagined that I'd be in this position—working alongside people I admired, respected, and who I knew needed my expertise. I was both grateful for the opportunity and, more importantly, no longer bogged down by the unnecessary complexities of the organization. Just the opportunity to support and push leaders to reimagine how to leverage their privilege, power, and responsibility to make change.

I finished up Thursday evening, which—coincidentally—was Valentine's Day. I went out for an early dinner alone, had a glass of wine, and watched TV.

DR. ROBIN MARTIN

Local news reported a looming threat of a winter storm in D.C., so I decided to leave early. I woke up the next morning, caught an Uber to the airport, and was determined to catch the first flight out—eager to avoid an unplanned weekend in Chocolate City. I love D.C.[1], but no one wants to get stuck there.

The airport lines were longer than usual. I waited patiently as the front desk attendant tried to check in a large group of international travelers.

Someone in the group noticed I was alone and asked if I wanted to jump the line. I gleefully said yes and thanked her for letting me check in ahead.

I approached the counter as the attendant checked flights back to Cincinnati. I smiled, hoping it might earn me some favor and get me on the first flight out.

My pretty smile didn't work this time. Despite arriving early, the attendant couldn't get me on the first flight. She offered to put me on standby for the next flight—

five hours later—and if that didn't work, I'd have to catch my original evening flight.

Disappointed, I hopped on the Metro and headed back to the Dupont Circle hotel where I'd stayed all week. My plan was to grab some breakfast, get some work done, and enjoy the city for a few more hours.

As I stood on the Metro platform, the sun beaming on my face, I felt happy and grateful. I whispered a simple prayer—thanking God and the universe for giving me the ability and opportunity to find my purpose in the work, and to support leaders making a real impact. That prayer of gratitude quickly turned into a prayer of surrender.

I spoke the following words aloud—*"God, I'll do what you ask of me. Whatever it is, I will say yes."*

The train arrived. I got on, rode three stops, transferred—nearly missed it—then two more stops and got off at Dupont Circle.

DR. ROBIN MARTIN

As I headed up the escalator, I saw a tall, dark, handsome guy. He turned once and looked at me— as if to confirm what he'd just seen. I noticed the double-take immediately.

I still had my N-95 mask on; I wasn't taking any chances with my health. As I reached the top of the escalator, I pulled the mask off—and there he was, standing there.

Waiting.

"Hello," he said.

"Hello," I replied.

"Who are you?" he asked.

"Excuse me?"

He introduced himself.

"My name is Ludovic," he said, with a thick French accent. Then, to my surprise, he said...

"Would you like to have coffee with me?"

NAVIGATING LOVE

"Huh?"

"Where are you headed? Maybe I can walk with you? Are you free for coffee?"

"Huh? Where?"

"I don't know this place. I'm from France—I don't know my way around here."

My mind was racing. I wanted to run. But something in me calmed. I heard that quiet voice again: "Say yes."

So, I did.

We walked across the street to the hotel and grabbed coffee. We talked for two hours.

He told me about his work, his dissertation, and that this was his first time in the U.S.

Coffee turned into lunch. Lunch turned into dinner at a Chinese restaurant. My fortune cookie at dinner read: "It's time to call your loved ones to share the wonderful news."

DR. ROBIN MARTIN

If I'm being honest, the day was a blur. I remember him leaning across the table, kissing me, and grabbing my hand like we had known each other for years. And somehow, inside, I was calm.

There was something about his spirit—a quiet sincerity that drew me in. At lunch, he talked about his mother, her death, and the impact it had on his life. His pain was palpable. So was his openness. I was surprised at how vulnerable he allowed himself to be. It was unexpected and welcomed.

Later, he asked me to stay. To delay my flight. To spend the night. I was both sure and unsure. I called my cousin and a good friend to track my location and check his background. I felt safe—but I wasn't taking any chances. I was going to be protected.

In control.

The next morning, we left D.C.—him to France, and me back to Cincinnati—wondering if I'd ever see him again.

NAVIGATING LOVE

Now safely back home, I called my cousin and my 'spy friend' and told them, *"I think he's the one."*

DR. ROBIN MARTIN

COURAGE CARD

Chapter 8

THE FIRST GOODBYE

My first trip to Lyon was an adventure. I didn't know what to expect, but I was ready for the endless possibilities. We had only known each other for three and a half weeks before I hopped on a plane to stay in France for a month. Before getting on that plane, we talked every day. Hours on WhatsApp getting to know each other. He shared more about his background—his previous marriage, his children, and his mother.

While I had the usual jitters about starting a new relationship, his presence brought me a calm I had never experienced with a man before. He was strong yet soft. Kind yet forceful. Vulnerable yet volatile. He was something entirely new for me.

DR. ROBIN MARTIN

When I arrived in France, my luggage did not. It took several days before I had clothes—not that it mattered much. We spent the first few days in bed. He had prepared dinner for me, with flowers on the table to welcome me into his home. I noticed every detail, every small effort to make me feel safe and cared for.

A few days later, he left for a 24-hour shift, and I was on my own. It was my first time in the city, and I didn't speak the language. But when the airline finally delivered my luggage, I set off with excitement. I love adventure. I love exploring new places, meeting new people, discovering new restaurants. As he worked tirelessly, I was wandering through this beautiful, unfamiliar city, finally tasting the gap year experience I had longed for.

When he returned home from work, he invited a few of his friends over to "check me out"—the "crazy American" he had met in DC. They were kind and warm, yet I could feel the quiet suspicion in the room. This was new for both of us. We had jumped off the side of the boat together, and no one—not even us—knew where we were swimming.

When he wasn't working, we took long walks, exploring together. One evening, we decided to stay in and order food. I remember the peace of that night—him sitting across the room, music filling the silence. I closed my eyes, inhaling the moment, letting myself fall into a light trance.

He walked across the room, took my hand, pulled me close—and we danced.

It had only been a few weeks, but they were glorious. And at that moment, I surrendered.

Until—

The final week of our stay, we had dinner with a friend. He had talked about him often, so I leaned in and tried to get to know his friend better. He was one of the few people I'd met so far who spoke English. Everyone else spoke French, so many nights I sat in silence—muted—

DR. ROBIN MARTIN

unable to fully participate in the conversations without him translating for me.

To be honest, I didn't mind the silence. Not knowing the language was a new experience, so the simple act of listening to sounds and inflection was enough. But after three weeks of silence, I wanted to talk to someone other than him.

At dinner, I was extra chatty with his friend. We talked about all kinds of things—his life, his family, his spiritual beliefs. He was friendly and kind. I remember staring at him and noticing his impeccably shaped eyebrows. I've always been secretly jealous of men with naturally manicured eyebrows and long eyelashes. Without hesitation, I looked straight into his friend's eyes and said, "You have beautiful eyebrows."

At that moment, I didn't notice the shift in Ludovic's body language. I was simply being nice.

We left the restaurant, and I grabbed my partner's hand, pressed my body against his. I had a great evening and wanted to show my gratitude—for the night, for the time, for him.

But when we got home, I noticed a shift. A certain coldness. I brushed it off.

I didn't sleep well that night. I tossed and turned. At one point, he awakened me with a gentle touch and asked if I was okay. Startled, I replied yes. "What happened?" I asked.

He said I had been calling his name and reaching for him in my sleep. Still confused and not fully awake, I drifted back to sleep.

The next morning, as he got ready for work, he kissed his forefingers, patted me on the head, and walked out the door. I sat on the edge of the bed, stunned.

"What the fuck was that?"

No words were spoken. It was the first time; I felt the emotional emptiness.

DR. ROBIN MARTIN

From the beginning of this romance, I had felt safe. He exuded confidence, calm, and kindness. I always felt secure around him.

Not now.

I couldn't explain what was happening. All I knew was his spirit had shifted, and I felt alone in a strange city.

The fairytale was coming to an end.

That day, while he was at work, I started looking up flights so I could return home earlier than planned. Just like my mother, I found myself whispering to my cousin: "I think I'm going to leave."

Later that day, he called just to check in. I could feel it—the coldness, the mundane tone.

I asked, "What's happening?"

"What do you mean?" he replied.

"Something shifted, and I'm not sure why."

"You disrespected me last night at dinner. I don't want to talk about this now, but we will when I get home."

"What? Ugh. I thought we had a great night."

"You ignored me at dinner. I wasn't included in the conversation. I just sat there watching you and him talk."

"I was just getting to know your friend…"

"Robin, I can't talk about this now. We'll talk tomorrow."

"Okay… bye."

The call ended, but my emotions were already racing—full speed down a four-lane highway.

For me, the dinner was the first time I had a conversation with another English speaker outside of him. It made me feel at home.

For him, it felt like rejection. Like I turned my attention elsewhere.

DR. ROBIN MARTIN

Two sides of the same story. Both true.

When he returned home, we didn't talk immediately. He started cooking lunch and making small talk.

To be honest, I didn't have time for small talk. Every hour, the price of the return ticket was going up, and my mind was racing. Look, dude—"let's just have the conversation so I can book this damn ticket and go. It was fun. But now, it's time to go."

We finally started talking. Both of us defended our positions. We expressed our concerns. Eventually, we apologized. Hugged. Had a great dinner. And moved on.

I stayed the rest of the week and returned home on my original flight.

But on the flight back, I couldn't shake that cold, heartless, disconnected feeling I'd had that morning. I kept thinking about the dream—calling his name in a panic and reaching for him in my sleep.

My plane landed. I was back home.

NAVIGATING LOVE

COURAGE CARD

Be Human: *To yearn for love is to Be Human.*

Be in Community/Interconnectedness: *To yearn to be loved in a community is Human.*

Be Curious: *To learn how to love is Human.*

Be Courageous: *To love and be loved takes Courage.*

Chapter 9

WHAT OUR MOTHERS TAUGHT US

Daily talks, deeper commitments, shared prayers—my next few trips back to France followed a similar pattern. Adventure, connection, laughter... followed by brief conflict, emotional breakdowns, and then more conversations.

I always admired how certain he was about us. As if he knew from the beginning that I was the one God had sent him.

I remember us walking down the street, hand in hand, and me wondering out loud about the magic of our story. The silent prayer I mumbled in the DC Metro

NAVIGATING LOVE

station—that "yes" I whispered into the universe—kept echoing. I turned to him, our hands tightly clasped, and said, "This is such a faith walk for me."

He paused, stopped walking, and replied, "I know what you mean intellectually. I understand what you're saying. But you need to know... I've moved beyond the feeling of shock. My heart and my head are aligned. You are the one."

Well, damn. I didn't have a response. I just walked in silence, letting his hand guide my body to whatever came next.

I had never been in a relationship where the man was so sure—so unafraid. He exuded a kind of sacred confidence. From the beginning, there was something in his spirit that seemed to know we were meant to be. Even amidst our struggles.

Me? I was always looking for a way out. A backup plan. An exit route. I was Gladys. A runner. Unhoused. A flight risk. And still...it never seemed to shake him. I must admit, his confidence both scared me and drew me in. And yet, even as I wrestled with my own restlessness, life kept pulling us forward.

We spent months planning his first trip back to the U.S. to meet my family and friends. I was a little nervous, but excited to host him on my own turf. I had spent so much time in France since we met that I wanted him to see me—the real me—in my own environment.

Before his arrival, mom and I talked about him every day.

When I told her I was in love, she lit up. She wanted to hear the story over and over again. "Tell me how you met," she'd say, grinning like a little girl. Given our recent rocky history, I couldn't fully explain the depth of her excitement. But she kept repeating, "You deserve this. Of all the people in the world, Robin—you deserve this."

She said it so many times, it made me uncomfortable. I wasn't sure why. Maybe because it felt like swallowing

NAVIGATING LOVE

a mouthful of fairy tale. But in that moment, I knew I had to take it in.

He arrived. We spent a few days in Cincinnati before driving down to meet Mom. I was nervous and excited.

When he walked into the house, it was love at first sight. She welcomed him with open arms. Over the next few days, there were dinners, joint pedicures, and a party where they danced, and even a sweet connection with my big brother. He was a hit. I felt proud—grounded in the possibility that maybe, just maybe, this was real.

Then it happened—before we left Knoxville, she spoke the magic phrase, her favorite mantra, the one she reserved only for family. She looked him in the eyes and said: "I love you. I bless you. I appreciate you."

Her joy was palpable.

A few months earlier, before his visit, I had taken a solo trip to visit her. We sat on the back porch while she

DR. ROBIN MARTIN

smoked a cigarette, her dementia-fogged mind holding onto rare clarity that day. She began, as she often did: "Tell me how you met again. I still can't believe it," she said, smiling. Then came the refrain I had heard so many times before: "You deserve this, Robin. You deserve this."

Then, she turned to me.

"Do you really love him, Robin?"

"Yes," I said. "I really love him."

"I'm so happy for you."

She was beaming.

I turned and looked at her and I asked a question I'd always wanted to ask:

"Have you ever been in love?"

Her face changed.

"No. I don't think I've ever been in love. It was all about a screw. I was raped."

NAVIGATING LOVE

She said it flat. Like a memory she'd filed away long ago.

"They catch you," she continued. "No dating. Just a rush. They'd rape me. I never had real feelings for a man. I got drunk, and the next thing I knew, he raped me. I didn't like them. They didn't like me. They just fucked me. Even your daddy. I didn't really like him either. We just fucked, and I got pregnant. We never really had a relationship." She stared ahead.

"When I look back on my life, I think—where the hell were *you*? It was like I wasn't even present in my own life. And in a way, I'm still that way. That's how I got all my children."

She paused, then continued.

"After the last baby, I prayed to the good Lord to help me raise my children. I asked Him not to let them live like me. And he did it. I'm so proud of you all. Everyone of you is successful in your own right."

I reached my hand towards her and said: "We are who we are because of you. You raised us well."

DR. ROBIN MARTIN

She took a drag from her cigarette.

"I'll always praise the Lord for my children. I was smart, Robin. I was in the National Honor Society. I had a scholarship to go to Spelman College. But my life went downhill after my daddy came home one day, beat my mother, shot up the house, and left. Still… God gave me a good life. From where I started. God has been good to me. I thank Him every day for my children. *He* did that."

She looked out at the trees, and we sat in silence.

She continued.

"That's when I started praying. Started going to church. I asked God to help me raise my kids. And He did. That's the biggest blessing in my life—even if they were from different men."

We sat silently for a few more minutes before I helped her up from the chair, and together we walked back inside the house.

That was a hard conversation. But I needed to hear it.

NAVIGATING LOVE

I learned so much about her.

And so much about me.

DR. ROBIN MARTIN

COURAGE CARD

Chapter 10

THE GRIEF IN THE YES

On the drive back from the visit, her words haunted me: *"When I look back on my life, I think—where the hell were you? It was like I wasn't even present in my own life. And in a way, I'm still that way."*

There was so much to unpack. I began to wonder how her relationship with her father had shaped her views about love, about men, about life.

How had her absence from her own life—her refusal, or maybe her inability, to be fully present—led her to keep running? From house to house, man to man... even now, well into her seventies.

DR. ROBIN MARTIN

And yet, I had never seen her so happy for me. I always knew she was proud, but this kind of joy—open, unguarded joy—was new. My love, in some strange way, became her home. Every time we spoke, she asked about him: "Tell Ludovic that I love him, I bless him, and I appreciate him."

She wanted me to repeat the story of how we met, again and again. In that story, she found life. It gave her something to hold on to—a different ending, maybe even a different beginning. She saw God's blessing in our love, a blessing she longed for but never had.

For Ludovic, my mother had become the mother presence he had missed in his own life. When he met her—and every time he spoke with my mother—his face lit up. Whenever she said, "I love you, I bless you, and I appreciate you," I could see the little boy in him soften. Her instant, unconditional love awakened something in him—as if it reminded him of what had always been missing, a space he too felt unhoused in.

NAVIGATING LOVE

Perhaps that's why he clung so tightly to her words—because in them he found echoes of the love and presence he still longed for from his own mother.

Every time he spoke about his own mother, there was a quiet grief in his voice, a deep longing. His eyes often welled as he described her death and the guilt he still carried: He often repeated— "I'm a doctor. I should've been there. I could have saved her."

And while he knew that wasn't true, somewhere deep inside he needed to believe it. That memory—that belief he could save, that he could control—I believe became the anchor that allowed him to function in a chaotic world as an emergency room physician. It fuels his purpose to save others, because it is the one moment he can still hold onto.

Yet holding so tightly to that belief also left a fracture. It gave him the uncanny ability to be both present and absent—deeply compassionate, yet strangely distant in the same breath. At work, that separation makes him extraordinary. At home, it casts a shadow—especially after a disagreement—arriving without warning: silence, emptiness, distance.

From the start, I could feel it—that cold, distant energy that would suddenly settle over him. Sometimes it followed a disagreement, but other times it arrived unannounced. No warning. Just silence. Emptiness. A shadow. And each time, I'd ask:

"What's happening?"

"Nothing," he would say.

"I feel disconnected from you."

"I'm fine, sweetie. Nothing's wrong."

But something was always wrong. I could feel it in my bones.

And when it happens, I often wondered if the emptiness was tied to his longing for his mother—to the little boy still grieving her absence. I've come to believe that his ability to disconnect wasn't always about me. At times, it wasn't about me at all. It was about survival. About the pain he has never been able to outrun.

The Proposal

After seven months into our courtship, he proposed. And I said yes.

He was always a planner. Trips, train rides, and what time we left the house. He was in charge of those details, and I loved not having to control them. It's funny how quickly I surrendered to him.

The night he proposed caught me off guard. We'd talked about marriage often, but I wasn't expecting it that evening.

He had planned dinner at a beautiful restaurant at the top of the city—nothing unusual for us. We both loved dressing up, eating well, and enjoying the moment.

I came out of the bedroom fully dressed and asked, "Which necklace do you like—this one, or this one?"

DR. ROBIN MARTIN

He picked the simpler one. I went back to the bathroom and put on the flashier one.

"I really liked the other one. Why did you change it?"

"I just like this one better."

"Then why did you ask my opinion?"

"It was just your opinion. I wanted to hear it, but I'm wearing the one I feel best in." I sensed his frustration. He let it go, but the frustration hung there between us.

Then, right before we walked out the door, he turned to me and said, "I need to ask you something."

He dropped to one knee and asked me to marry him.

I said yes.

The evening was perfect. The food, the view, his eyes locked on mine. I was happy.

Until—

NAVIGATING LOVE

In the middle of the night, I woke up and stared at the ceiling. Something was rising in me that I didn't understand. Tears started streaming down my face. I felt a deep, overwhelming sadness.

He was asleep beside me, and suddenly panic rose in my chest. My mind raced, searching for something steady to hold onto. I turned to the Framework—Be Curious—and began asking myself questions to make sense of the moment.

What are you really feeling?

Do you want to marry this man?

Are you happy?

Yes, I wanted to marry him. Yes, I was happy. Then it hit me: I was grieving.

It was the beginning of mourning the life I had built and loved.

DR. ROBIN MARTIN

I'd been happily single for a long time. I was never the girl dreaming of a big wedding or a house full of kids. I was the runner. The free bird. I moved as I pleased.

That kind of freedom—real or imagined—was changing. And I had to give it a proper burial.

So, I lay beside him and cried myself back to sleep.

Over the next few days, I shared the good news with friends and family... and cried at night.

I was never in doubt about us. I just needed space to mourn my life as I knew it. To grieve the quiet, personal freedom I had protected for so long.

I thought about that moment with the necklace. I thought about his small frustration and how I'd never had to explain myself like that before.

My "singleness" showed up—bold, loud—and tried to strangle me.

And in that moment, I realized—

Even joy has grief.

NAVIGATING LOVE

Even freedom has a cost.

And even love requires letting go.

DR. ROBIN MARTIN

COURAGE CARD: WORDS FROM THE WOMAN KING

The Woman King

We fight or we die,

No children, no husband— Here, I

stand as the hunter, Not the prey.

It is play, but it is war.

We are your family now.

They try to stab me. I stab them back.

There will be no prisoners.

Burn it to the ground.

This is how we survive.

Tell me the dream—

"In the jungle, something lurks in the darkness,

NAVIGATING LOVE

A beast. I can smell its sweat and fear."

Fire whispers: "Someone from your past? Go to the altar, and gifts will be there." Welcome to the

King's Guard,

Where the devil's mark burns bright,

Not as a curse,

But as a crown.

The beast I seek—it's me.

I silenced her, denied her pain.

But no longer.

I am going to heal now.

You survived because you were meant to be here.

Chapter 11

DON'T LEAVE ME WHILE YOU'RE STILL HERE

Throughout the course of our courtship, we faced challenges. Some were cultural. Others were about language, communication, and personality. And sometimes, it was simply the reality of two smart, passionate people in love—where intellectual sparring could feel like a sexy Game of Thrones, with someone destined to win. Or worse, where someone was bound to lose.

When I tell people our story, they gush—imagining a perfect, idyllic fairytale romance, untouched by struggle. But I always remind them:

NAVIGATING LOVE

Love and rage are so deeply intertwined that the naked eye fails to discern between the two.

I love this man with everything in my soul. We fit. The universe brought us together to teach us—he and I—about ourselves. And it took me a long time to realize that the tension, the flare-ups, the silence weren't just "relationship problems"—they were each of us doing our individual work—our spiritual work—sometimes clumsily, sometimes painfully, always human.

One of the clearest examples of that tension came in New Orleans.

I was so excited. A festival. Music. Good food. Dancing. I was ready to wild out. He was more reserved. There has always been a tension between us: my free, adventurous spirit—where plans feel irrelevant—against his more conservative nature, where plans are fixed and total freedom feels dangerous, even insecure.

This was his first time in the city, so he seemed to be easily overwhelmed, and happy to eat and hang out in

DR. ROBIN MARTIN

the hotel room. I never saw his discomfort. I was too busy trying to relive the excitement I had the previous year, before I met him. I was recapturing my freedom, so we moved through the trip like strangers with different itineraries.

When we got back to Cincinnati, I carried a quiet resentment. I hadn't enjoyed myself. Little did I know, he was also harboring his own frustrations—about something I had done.

But instead of talking about it, an Antarctic wind filled the air. Cold. Still. Silent.

So I asked:

"What's happening?"
"Nothing."
"I feel disconnected from you."
"I'm fine, sweetie."

I knew something was wrong. That night, I tried to draw him close. He chose the other room. Watched TV. I fell asleep in the bed alone.

NAVIGATING LOVE

It was our last night together in the city, and I felt abandoned.

The next morning, I woke early, made coffee, and helped him pack.

We drove to the airport in silence.

I parked. Walked him in and waited while he checked his bags.

I hoped we could talk. Even for five minutes. But he refused. Said he needed to get to his gate. He pecked me on the lips and walked away.

I was broken.

I held back tears as I walked to the car, unsure where to turn or who to call.

Hell, I didn't even know what had just happened.

Then came the rush. The rage.

Fuck you.

DR. ROBIN MARTIN

If you're fine, great. Be fine. But I'm out of here. If I have to do this alone again, I will.

I've done it before.

By the time I got home, I had mentally left the relationship.

Robin had left the building.

The next few weeks were a blur. We barely spoke. My body was still in the relationship, but my mind had packed up and left. This felt comfortable- familiar.

Leaving was familiar.

It came with a kind of freedom I understood.

And just like my mother, I had the uncanny ability to "fuck and leave them."

I was never a clingy woman. I didn't do breakdowns.

I could count on one hand how many times I'd cried over a man.

NAVIGATING LOVE

I always kept a wall up—just in case. My bags were always packed.

But this time... this time was different.

The wall was still there, but it wasn't made of brick. It was thinner. Maybe paper.

Maybe glass.

It took months for us to find our way back.

And even then, I struggled to trust him.

I didn't trust that he wouldn't disappear. Leave me emotionally stranded—again.

When he went cold, it unsteadied me.

And before I let someone destabilize me again, I'd rather leave first.

I'd rather be the one to walk.

Love and rage are so deeply intertwined that the naked eye fails to discern between the two.

DR. ROBIN MARTIN

Over the next few months, we slowly worked our way back to each other.

Chapter 12

TRAGIC FAIRY ENCOUNTER

Have you ever been so angry at another person that you could imagine them lying in the street, hurt, and you walk right past—without lifting a finger to help?

If not, welcome to my world.

I like to think that my educated, sensitive, caring self is always present. But fuck—that's not the full story. Under the right circumstances, I can be mean.

Heartless. Vicious. We all can.

I could feel something brewing earlier in the week, so I tried to avoid the fallout.

DR. ROBIN MARTIN

He was scheduled to work in another city for a few days when a friend called and asked if I wanted to hop on a plane and visit them in another country. Just for four days.

Without hesitation, I was in. My bags were already packed and the ticket booked before I even mentioned it to him. The only thing left was to "ask" him if it was okay to go—knowing damn well I didn't want a discussion, just agreement.

But the conversation didn't go the way I'd imagined it in my head. Honestly, I hadn't really thought about how he might feel. In my mind, it was simple: he'd be working all week, and I'd be stuck alone in a hotel. Hanging out with my friends, seeing a new place—that wasn't just the best option. It was the only option.

But he had other plans.

He wanted me to come with him on the work trip. I'd only been in France for a week, and he wanted to simply spend time together—even if it was limited.

NAVIGATING LOVE

We talked, but not really. The words were there, but the connection wasn't.

At that moment, I chose to isolate myself. He always wanted me near—close enough to feel, close enough to touch. But I often failed to appreciate that yearning. I was becoming his peace, yet I kept running—still unsure of how to truly share my life, how to tune myself to another person's needs. I didn't see it then, but for him, my distance must have felt like rejection. Like being left alone. Unseen.

He grew upset. And I retreated into the only place I knew—being the lone-wolf Robin.

So when the choice came, I went nowhere. I didn't go with my friends. I didn't go with him. Instead, I stayed at the house—alone, exactly where my isolation had already placed me.

He packed his things. No kiss goodbye. No "I love you." He just left.

DR. ROBIN MARTIN

The silence. The emotional distance. The coldness. The way we both left felt cruel.

I spent the next three days raging—trying to figure out how I was going to tell everyone it was over.

Just months after he proposed, I had posted our story on Facebook—shared it with friends, family, and the world. It was the first time in my life that I let people see me this vulnerable, especially about love. The outpouring of joy and support was overwhelming. Old friends, new friends, strangers...everyone wanted to believe in our story.

I was especially struck by how many Black women reached out to me. They said our story gave them something they hadn't felt in a long time—hope, joy, magic, and the belief that possibility still existed. That maybe, just maybe, love was still waiting somewhere out there for them, too.

We had become a symbol. A fairy tale. And our story no longer just belonged to us—it belonged to them.

And here I was... angry as hell. Wanting to burn it all to the ground.

The truth.
If you give me three days to rage unchecked, it can turn tragic.
But I had told too many people.
Too many people had invested their joy in our joy.
Too many people were watching.
And somewhere inside that fire, I sat down on the edge of the bed and wrote this:

Tragic Fairy Encounter

What happens when a fairy tale encounter begins to feel tragic?
Do you let go, carrying with you the lessons needed for the next chapter?
Or do you stay—hoping that this love won't destroy the very thing the universe has called forth in you: courage?

DR. ROBIN MARTIN

I no longer yearn to be understood.
I simply want to be—to exist.
Approval is a costly debt I'm no longer willing to pay at this stage in my life.

I am whole.
I came here whole.
And I will leave this earth whole.
That is my destiny—my divine inheritance.

This relationship has moved me beyond the impulse to run or avoid hard things. It has given me the courage to stay, even in the midst of uncertainty and conflict. And still, it has given me the power to recognize the difference between *leaving* and *running*.

Leaving is a choice.
Running was my cowardly attempt to escape pain or the fear of abandonment.
Maybe this love has taught me that.
Maybe it has shown me the quiet strength in choosing to walk away—not out of fear, but from self-respect.

NAVIGATING LOVE

Today, I contemplated leaving.
Not because I'm afraid—
But because I am committed to honoring myself.
It is my responsibility to ensure that my humanity is centered, seen, and loved at all times.
I cannot and will not hand over that responsibility to anyone else.
That is my work to do—and I must do it well.

When the fairy tale begins to feel tragic,
I choose to pause, reassess, and remember my own humanity.
Because losing myself to uphold the illusion of a fairy tale wouldn't just feel tragic— It *would be* tragic.

DR. ROBIN MARTIN

COURAGE CARD

Chapter 13

I WILL TRY MY BEST

When I first started writing the last chapter, it was all about him. He was the problem. The blame. The reason things went south. Despite so many months of joy, happiness, and sheer pleasure, I wanted so badly for this to come to an end. Too afraid to accept that I had found the love of my life. A friend to share this life with.

But then the words started to shift—taking shape into another episode of Runaway Robin.

And while that didn't leave him blameless, it forced me to center myself in the chaos and stop playing the victim.

Days before my birthday, we fought.

DR. ROBIN MARTIN

We had planned a beautiful trip to Morocco to celebrate my birthday. The bags were packed, flights booked, and reservations made at a five-star hotel. And then—another explosion.

He came home the day before we were supposed to leave. Before his arrival, he called and asked if we could talk.

When he walked through the door, it felt like I was meeting a stranger. I didn't want him to touch me. I didn't want him near me.

Out of anger, I had removed a framed photo of myself from the living room. He noticed it immediately.

We exchanged sharp words. Fireworks exploded. It was a full-on intellectual war. His voice rose. Mine followed. Around and around we went.

What he didn't know was that I had already made alternate plans to fly to Morocco—alone—if we couldn't resolve things. I had booked another flight. I was going to have a great birthday—with or without him.

Then he looked me straight in the eyes and asked, "Are you going to leave?"

I stumbled. I felt exposed. That was supposed to be my card to play, but like a casino dealer, he called my hand.

"Yes. I was planning to leave. I don't feel safe," I answered.

"Robin," he said, "we had a disagreement. We can work through this. This isn't something to leave over."

He looked down—depleted, resigned and said— "If you want to leave, I can't stop you. I've been left before. I can't make anyone stay. But I hope you don't go."

I told him that while I may have been planning to leave physically, his emotional absence felt like abandonment, too. He didn't walk out the door— but he disappeared all the same.

We started to spiral again. Same road. Same patterns.

DR. ROBIN MARTIN

Then, suddenly, I saw it. I started to see the damage in his eyes. My constant threats of leaving reopened wounds—memories of his mother's absence, and the fractures in his relationship with his estranged ex-wife and children. What I thought was leverage was actually salt poured into unhealed scars. My threats weren't low blows—they were killing blows. I could see that more clearly now, maybe for the first time.

Then I asked a simple question: *"Do we want to be right, or do we want to get this right?"*

There was a long silence. Then, slowly, we both softened. The pain was still there, but we were willing to try.

He took the first step. He didn't promise perfection—he promised effort. He said he would seek counseling to understand why he shut down emotionally. And I, in turn, promised to seek counseling myself and not threaten to leave every time things got hard.

NAVIGATING LOVE

Even with the storm still overhead, we chose to begin again. To recommit to each other in a more intentional way. We chose love.

Before I went to bed that night, I wrote:

"Today, your trigger triggered my trigger—instantly leaving us suspended in the toilet like a pile of shit trying to go down a small drain, whirling around aimlessly waiting for the thrust and weight of the water to force it into the sewage.

The pain and feelings of betrayal hit all at once, like a thousand tiny cuts with nowhere to run. My instinct was to flee—but this time, there was no open door.

So, I sat beside you, my bags packed, hoping I wouldn't suffocate from your deadly trigger: "shutting down." Emotional abandonment. A shield you use, not just to protect yourself from me, but from the world.

DR. ROBIN MARTIN

We both ran towards the familiar—our homes away from home. You, emotionally shutting down. I, physically running away - isolating myself from everything.

Then you said, "I will try my best." I don't promise that we will never have issues or fight; however, I will make every effort not to shut down or make you feel unsafe." You didn't make promises. You just offered truth.

You looked me in the eyes and said it again, slower: 'I will try my best.' I had never heard those words from a man before. No grand gesture. No sweeping apology. Just you—human, honest, trying. And that was enough."

That night, I fell deeper in love.

We went to bed. And the next day, we flew to Morocco.

NAVIGATING LOVE

COURAGE CARD: THE LITTLE BOY

I love the little boy in you. Your slanted, mischievous smile when a witted thought crosses the cerebral cortex, waiting to be unleashed from your lips into the universe.

I love the little boy in you. The way insecurity shows up as you gently pull back your soul, inwardly and silently retreating to protect yourself.

I love the little boy in you. Yearning to be spooned by my warm body and fiery breath on your neck.

I love watching the little boy when you're around your friends and family. You lead, you learn, you work. The way you care for others' thoughts, their contributions, their gifts. Giving high praise.

I love the little boy because the grown man allows him to live freely inside.

I love when the father and the son become one.

Chapter 14

BENIN — THE TRIP THAT CHANGED EVERYTHING

We took our first trip to his home country, Benin. I had never been to West Africa. I landed early in the morning in Ghana, where he was working on a project. From there, the plan was to travel through Togo, and then into Benin to spend time with his family.

One of his younger sisters came to Ghana to pick us up. At first, I didn't understand why this was necessary—until we reached the national border stops. The extortion, the endless bribes, the chaotic checkpoints just to cross from one country into another—it was eye-opening and, if I'm honest, a little traumatic for me.

NAVIGATING LOVE

By the time we finally arrived at his house in Benin, I was exhausted.

The next morning—and every morning after—felt like a revelation. Benin was beautifully different. It was industrious, fast-moving, crowded, and hot. Paved roads tangled with dirt ones. Wealth and poverty intertwined. My head was on a constant swivel. I was a wide-eyed tourist, delighted to take it all in.

Weeks before the trip, he decided we would stay in his childhood home rather than in a hotel. That choice changed everything.

From the bathroom window, I saw a new world unfold each day: men and young boys repairing cars, children laughing and playing in the streets, baby goats and free-range chickens darting between homes, girls in groups walking to school, mothers and fathers balancing groceries or bags on their heads. What some might call poverty, I saw as ingenuity and resilience— an industrious people making life work with what God had given them.

DR. ROBIN MARTIN

Each day, we gathered for breakfast and dinner with his elder sisters. They cooked with care, made sure our needs were met, and even pressed my clothes with a tenderness I wasn't used to receiving. I had never known that kind of care. I had always been the one cooking, caring, holding everything together. For the first time, I allowed myself simply to receive.

It was also the first time I saw him fully within his family unit—not just as my partner, but as their brother, their anchor. He was the man of the house, the most successful, the one everyone trusted and leaned on. In many ways, he was the "me" of his family. I could see the pride he carried in that role, but I also sensed the burden—the weight of always being the one.

Watching him in that role—the pillar everyone leaned on, made me wonder where that strength came from. And then I noticed the large portraits of his parents resting on the floor, waiting to be hung. His mother's face dominated the room: strong, dignified, stern yet

NAVIGATING LOVE

inviting. Her upright shoulders and steady gaze spoke of confidence and certainty.

From the stories his sisters told, it was clear she was the center of the family, the one everyone revered. She had built a business that sustained her children even beyond her death. I still wonder if he sees traces of her in me.

Being in his childhood home also stirred memories of my own father, and the ways he and my partner seemed to mirror one another. I saw it in his kindness, his quiet strength, even in the rhythm of his walk and the way he moved his arms. Echoes of my father lived in him. His tender yet steady way of seeing the world, his careful attention to details, the pride in preparing for our visit, the way he looked at me with honor—all of it reminded me of the man who first showed me what love, and dignity could look like.

When I first told a few close friends that I was dating an African man, many of them—subtly and not so subtly—warned me about the misogyny they believed African

DR. ROBIN MARTIN

men carried. They told me to be cautious, to watch for his need to control, for old beliefs about the woman's place in the home.

But sitting at the table with him and his older sisters, I saw something altogether different—the things I had come to love in him.

In our relationship, he valued my intellect. He saw it not as a threat, but as a strength—something to partner with, not compete against. My loud opinions, my certainty, my insistence on being heard never unsettled him. He welcomed them with curiosity, sometimes with playful debate, always with a desire to sharpen—not silence—my voice.

Watching him in his own environment, surrounded by the people who really knew him, who loved him unconditionally, and who wanted nothing more than to see him happy, forever changed how I saw him, how I saw family, and how I saw myself in relation to both.

Chapter 15

THE CIGARETTE

Once he and I made the commitment to work on our differences and fully lean into the relationship, the world opened up. I finally unpacked my bags—for good—and settled into knowing, believing, and trusting that he would become my forever home.

Over the next few months, I began to rediscover myself. I saw him more clearly. I learned how to address our differences without running. I learned how to love myself and love him at the same time.

And yet, even in our moments of growth and tenderness, my mother's presence lingered—lurking, watching, hovering in the background of every decision I made.

DR. ROBIN MARTIN

Every chance I got, I traveled—back and forth—between being with my partner and her. The emotional weight of whether she was okay started to take its toll.

He noticed the strain but never pressed. He understood that the mother-daughter relationship was sacred ground—one not to tread on without invitation. Instead, he also leaned in. He supported me. He gave me space to be there for her every time I asked.

If I'm being honest, I was just as dependent on her as she was on me. That dependence bound us together, even as it pulled us in different directions. She was walking her own tightrope—wanting me to come home more often, but also quietly hoping I would fly. Move across the world with this man who, in her eyes, was giving me a happiness she had never known. She wanted both things: for me to stay close, and for me to go far.

We both knew a choice had to be made.

NAVIGATING LOVE

So every time I went to France, I cleared my schedule to be with her. And every time I returned to the States, I cleared my calendar to be with her.

Most of our time together was spent during her smoke breaks. Still living with my brother, she spent much of her day alone. Her eyesight had deteriorated badly. Most of her world now lived in shadows. I could feel her fear of falling, of fading.

It scared me.

Just the thought of her going blind sent waves of helplessness and anger through me. I wanted to go back in time, to fix it—or at least give us a fighting chance to delay what felt inevitable.

So I kept the peace and showed up the best way I could.

One day, during one of our daily walks, she called. I looked at him and said, "It's my mom." He nodded. "Take it." So I answered, holding the phone close, and stayed with her as she made her way onto the back deck, then back inside and up the stairs safely into her room.

DR. ROBIN MARTIN

That night, I wrote:

The Cigarette

As the days began to wind down, your strength weakened, and fear began to settle in.

Our daily conversations increased—the impetus: the cigarette.

Your old habit.

At the age of 20, in an act of rebellion, you picked up what would become a 60-year ritual—never letting it go. It was the only constant in your life. The way you held that fiery vessel between your two fingers, gently caressing and inhaling every morsel of smoke into your lungs—I could see the relief, the comfort... and also the disgust. A quiet resentment for a habit that had, over the years, bred isolation.

Admittedly, I hated the smoking. The toxic fumes. The immediate headaches it triggered. The way secondhand toxins crept into my sphere. For years, I created separate spaces for you to enjoy those moments alone.

But distance—combined with the panic in your voice as you stood once again on the back porch, isolated—beckoned me to sacrifice.

Like clockwork, the phone rang.

9:30 a.m. for the first cigarette.

1:00 p.m. for the second.

5:00 p.m. for the final drag.

Somehow, God allowed me to hear the fear in your voice—inviting me to see this time as a gift.

Phone rings.

Mom: "You busy?"

Me: "I'm not too busy for you."

Mom: "Can you talk to me while I go out for a smoke?"

DR. ROBIN MARTIN

Me: "Yes."

Mom: "Thank you, Robin. You are my favorite friend."
Me: "Flattery will get you everywhere," I'd say.

And we'd laugh in unison.

The conversations never lasted more than ten minutes. Just enough time for you to inhale the smoke, ask about my partner, and talk about the weather. Just enough time for you to feel safe, alone on the back porch.

As time passed, I began to anticipate the call. That bad habit became a gift from God. It brought us closer. More importantly, it gave me space to heal. Space to sit with my own wounds. My regrets. Our regrets.

The cigarette gave us time to say goodbye. And every morsel of smoke that weakened you, strengthened us.

COURAGE REFLECTION

Her life is a tapestry of pain and love, trauma and resilience, and above all, immense courage.

To unearth my own authentic self, I must look into her soul and bear witness to her pain. It is not an easy task; it demands honesty, patience, and the willingness to see what I would rather avoid. But this is the path—the only path—that leads to freedom.

Courage is not about fixing or erasing the past. It is about standing in the truth of what has been, holding it with compassion, and choosing to live differently.

Chapter 16

THE SPACE BETWEEN LEAVING AND BECOMING

I took one last visit to see her before heading back to France for the summer. I could feel the anxiety—gravity tugging at my heart, mind, and soul. As I wrote the above passage, my words reminded me how love and pain can live side by side, and how often I've had to hold both. It was a kind of double consciousness, caught between the old truth and the new one—my old life, and the possibility of a new one.

As I began packing the house—folding winter clothes, cleaning rooms, and filling three suitcases—I came

NAVIGATING LOVE

across a letter my mother had written to me. A birthday letter. I'm not sure which birthday it was or how long it had been buried in those papers, but there it was—like a message sent by God.

It read:

Happy Birthday Robin,

I've never been good at giving gifts, so I decided to write you a letter for your birthday to tell you how much I love you.

I remember the day you were born. It was snowing really badly, and we almost didn't make it to the hospital in time. I prayed all day that you would wait until the weather cleared, but you had your own way and your own timing—just like you always have.

When you were first born, I would try to lay you on my chest and rock you to sleep. But every time I did, you would start squirming and fussing until I placed you beside me. That's when you settled, as if you already

DR. ROBIN MARTIN

knew how to find your own way. That's when I knew you would be independent.

I remember one Christmas when I didn't have any money to buy gifts. I told y'all to pray that God would send us some money. You looked me straight in the eyes, full of sincerity and optimism, and said, "I have an idea—why don't we ask God for a trillion dollars, that way we won't ever have to ask Him again." I knew right then you were a child who would always find a way out of no way. You have always been such a go-getter.

Anytime somebody needed something done, you would raise your hand and say, "I can do it." You were always taking charge, always believing in yourself, adventurous and fearless.

These are just a few of the gifts God has blessed you with—and through you, He has blessed me too. So on this birthday, I just wanted to share this gift with you, Robin. You see, you are the gift. You are my gift. Love You.

Happy Birthday

NAVIGATING LOVE

Mom

I sat outside in the heat of the summer sun reading the letter and cried. Every word touched my soul. That letter reminded me of her—of us—beyond our collective trauma, past the emotional highs and lows, beyond the leaving and the returning. It felt like something new was being born in me, a truth I could no longer ignore. It allowed me to release any remaining doubt about her love for me.

She has always been my friend. My biggest supporter. She knew me. She loved me. And despite the hard times, I never once questioned that love. Maybe we questioned its form. Maybe we got lost in the pain sometimes. But her love was always there—quiet and consistent like breath. The letter was a reminder that even in chaos, love endures.

And yet, love is never just one thing. It carries contradictions. It holds joy and grief, rage and courage, all at once. That tension lives inside me too. It is what

DR. ROBIN MARTIN

Du Bois called double consciousness—the ability, or maybe the burden, of holding two opposing truths at the same time. You don't escape either reality; you live inside both. You hold them in each hand—until the edges start to fray, and you're forced to loosen your grip on one in order to grasp the other with clarity and conviction.

So, with each passing day, I knew this was going to be my greatest test.
I needed to let go.
I needed to run toward love. Toward the man who had become my home.
He was my friend, my lover, my future—the one person I could share my deepest fears with. The one I could trust with the silent parts of me. The one who didn't flinch.

So, as the world became more violent and uncertain, I knew it was time to leave the comfort of what I knew—not just physically, but emotionally.

NAVIGATING LOVE

This wasn't a goodbye.
It was a psychological departure.
I had to stop mothering the mother.
Stop trying to solve every problem.
Stop worrying if she'd be okay.

I had to love her differently. More completely.
I had to trust the God who had always protected her—
even from the beginning.

Once I surrendered the urge to control her life—once I trusted that she was going to be okay—I turned my attention back to myself. I gave myself permission to be in love. To begin again.

My relationship and love for him started like a blazing star, fast and bright. But with time, it became something quieter—like consistent summer days, where the sun shines and the night falls gently. We had settled into each other, even through the hard times.

I knew I loved him. I just didn't know what that meant fully—only that he had become the center of my life. The one I wanted to care for, tend to, and pray for daily.

DR. ROBIN MARTIN

So, I packed up the house.
I packed up my life.
And I settled my mind, body, and spirit.
I am moving to France to be with my future husband.
I don't know exactly where this road leads…
But I know the rebirthing process begins again—with COURAGE.

THE END

NAVIGATING LOVE

A MEMOIR OF RAGE, COURAGE,
AND BECOMING

By Dr. Robin Martin

In a world that often demands our strength but rarely makes room for our softness, *Navigating Love* is a raw, honest, and powerful meditation on what it means to lead with humanity. In this first volume of the *Navigating Courage* series, Dr. Robin Martin invites readers into a deeply personal journey—of caregiving and grieving, of falling in love and letting go, of choosing courage when rage feels like the only option.

Grounded in the African philosophy of Ubuntu—"I am because you are"—this book weaves personal narrative, poetry, and powerful reflections through the lens of the Navigating Courage Framework: Be Human, Be in Community, Be Curious, and Be Courageous.

DR. ROBIN MARTIN

This is not a traditional love story. It is a love letter to Black women, to those caring for aging parents while building new lives, and to anyone standing at the intersection of heartbreak and transformation. *Navigating Love* is both a mirror and a map—offering readers space to feel, reflect, and rise.

www.ingramcontent.com/pod-product-compliance
Lightning Source LLC
Chambersburg PA
CBHW070851050426
42453CB00012B/2139